Introduction to Cloud Computing with AWS

Master Amazon Web Services for Cloud Development and Deployment

Greyson Chesterfield

COPYRIGHT

DISCLAIMER

The information provided in this book is for general informational purposes only. All content in this book reflects the author's views and is based on their research, knowledge, and experiences. The author and publisher make no representations or warranties of any kind concerning the completeness, accuracy, reliability, suitability, or availability of the information contained herein.

This book is not intended to be a substitute for professional advice, diagnosis, or treatment. Readers should seek professional advice for any specific concerns or conditions. The author and publisher disclaim any liability or responsibility for any direct, indirect, incidental, or consequential loss or damage arising from the use of the information contained in this book.

Contents

Chapter 1: What is Cloud Computing?

1.1 The Evolution from Traditional Servers to the Cloud

Begin with a relatable introduction about how businesses managed IT infrastructure in the past:

- **Traditional IT Setup**:
    - Companies purchased physical servers and built data centers.
    - Challenges: High upfront costs, underutilized resources, and scalability limitations.
    - Analogy: Compare owning a personal generator for electricity vs. using a utility grid.

- **Virtualization Era**:
    - The rise of virtual machines allowed better utilization of server resources.
    - Introduction of efficiency but still required on-premise management.

- **The Leap to the Cloud**:
    - Cloud computing emerged as a paradigm shift: pay only for what you use, and scale effortlessly.
    - Example: Discuss how startups no longer need massive IT investments to launch apps.

1.2 Definition of Cloud Computing and Its Characteristics

Provide a simple, jargon-free definition:

Cloud Computing: The on-demand delivery of IT resources (like servers, storage, databases, and software) over the internet with pay-as-you-go pricing.

Explain its core **characteristics**:

1. **Scalability**: Ability to scale up or down based on demand.

    o Example: An e-commerce site during Black Friday can handle increased traffic without downtime.

2. **Elasticity**: Automatically adjust resources to match workloads.

3. **Cost Efficiency**: Pay for only what you use (no need for idle infrastructure).

4. **Accessibility**: Access resources from anywhere via the internet.

5. **Reliability**: High uptime and redundancy with global data centers.

1.3 Real-World Example: How Netflix Leverages Cloud Computing

Discuss Netflix as a tangible example:

- **Problem Netflix Faced**: In the early 2000s, Netflix experienced outages due to the limitations of physical data centers.

- **Transition to AWS**:

  - Migrated infrastructure to AWS for streaming services.

  - Scaled globally to meet varying demands.

  - Launched personalized recommendations using AWS's machine learning tools.

- Outcome: Seamless streaming to millions of users worldwide, even during peak traffic like "Stranger Things" premieres.

Highlight how this success story embodies cloud computing's potential.

1.4 Types of Cloud Computing

Introduce the three main cloud deployment models:

1. **Public Cloud**:

   - Definition: Services offered over the internet and shared among multiple organizations.

   - Example: AWS, Microsoft Azure, Google Cloud.

   - Use Case: Startups using AWS to host their applications without buying servers.

2. **Private Cloud**:

   ○ Definition: Cloud infrastructure dedicated to a single organization.

   ○ Example: Banks and healthcare companies maintaining their own private clouds for data security.

   ○ Use Case: A hospital creating a private cloud to store patient records securely.

3. **Hybrid Cloud**:

   ○ Definition: Combines public and private clouds for flexibility.

   ○ Example: A company using a private cloud for sensitive data and public cloud for less critical operations.

   ○ Use Case: Media companies handling content rendering on public clouds but storing master files privately.

Provide an easy-to-remember analogy for these types:

Think of cloud models like transportation: Public buses (public cloud), personal cars (private cloud), and ride-sharing (hybrid cloud).

1.5 The Need for Cloud Services

Explain why cloud services are no longer a luxury but a necessity:

- **Modern Business Demands**: Faster innovation cycles and unpredictable workloads.

- **Global Access**: Workforce and customers are distributed worldwide, requiring always-on availability.

- **Cost Management**: Avoid upfront hardware investments.

- **Digital Transformation**:
    - Businesses transitioning to remote work.
    - Emerging technologies like IoT, AI/ML, and data analytics thrive in the cloud.

Example:

Imagine a small online retailer launching during a holiday season. With traditional infrastructure, they would need to over-purchase servers in advance. With the cloud, they can simply scale up during sales and scale down after, saving significant costs.

Chapter 2: Introduction to Amazon Web Services (AWS)

2.1 What is AWS? History and Market Dominance

Begin with a clear and concise definition of AWS:

Amazon Web Services (AWS) is a cloud computing platform offered by Amazon that provides a broad range of services, including computing power, storage, databases, networking, and machine learning, all delivered on-demand via the internet.

A Brief History of AWS:

- **Origins (2006)**:
    - AWS started as an internal infrastructure to support Amazon's retail business.
    - Launched as a public cloud service to address the broader market's IT infrastructure needs.

- **Milestones**:
  - **2008**: Introduction of Elastic Compute Cloud (EC2) and Simple Storage Service (S3).
  - **2012**: AWS hosts large-scale events like Netflix's streaming services.
  - **2020s**: Continued expansion into AI/ML, IoT, and quantum computing.

Market Dominance:

- AWS was the **first mover** in cloud computing, establishing an early lead.
- Commands a significant share of the market, competing with **Microsoft Azure** and **Google Cloud**.
- Trustworthy and widely adopted by enterprises like NASA, Airbnb, and healthcare providers.

2.2 Key Advantages of AWS

1. Cost-Effectiveness:

- **Pay-as-you-go model**: Users only pay for the resources they consume, reducing upfront costs.
- No need for purchasing hardware, maintenance, or upgrades.
- Example: A small business can deploy a website for as little as a few dollars a month.

2. Global Reach:

- AWS has data centers in **multiple Regions and Availability Zones** across the globe.
- Ensures low latency, high availability, and disaster recovery capabilities.
- Example: A global e-commerce platform can deliver consistent experiences to users worldwide.

3. Wide Range of Services:

- AWS offers over **200 services**, including:
  - **Compute** (EC2, Lambda),
  - **Storage** (S3, EFS, Glacier),
  - **Databases** (RDS, DynamoDB),
  - **Networking** (VPC, CloudFront).
- Example: A gaming company can host servers, store game data, and analyze player metrics—all within AWS.

4. Scalability and Elasticity:

- Easily scale applications up or down based on demand.
- Example: A ticketing platform can handle traffic spikes during event sales without downtime.

5. Security and Compliance:

- Built-in encryption, compliance with regulations (GDPR, HIPAA), and tools like Identity and Access Management (IAM) ensure secure usage.

2.3 Real-World Example: How Startups Use AWS to Scale Applications

Example: Airbnb

- **Problem**: In its early days, Airbnb faced fluctuating traffic patterns.

- **Solution**: By adopting AWS, Airbnb scaled its infrastructure to handle growth without upfront server investments.

- **Benefits**:

    ○ Rapid scalability to serve millions of users globally.

    ○ Cost management through AWS's pay-as-you-go model.

    ○ Leveraged AWS S3 for hosting user-uploaded images.

Other Startup Examples:

- **Slack**: Used AWS to enable real-time messaging and scale its global infrastructure.

- **Zocdoc**: Leveraged AWS to manage sensitive healthcare data securely.

Highlight how AWS empowers small teams to innovate without worrying about infrastructure.

2.4 Overview of AWS Free Tier and Pricing Model

AWS Free Tier

Introduce the AWS Free Tier as an entry point for readers to get hands-on experience:

- **What It Includes**:
  - **12-month Free Tier**:
    - EC2: 750 hours of compute time/month.
    - S3: 5GB of free storage.
    - RDS: 750 hours of database use/month.
  - **Always Free**:
    - Lambda: 1 million free requests/month.
    - CloudWatch: 10 custom metrics and basic monitoring.
- **Benefits**:
  - Ideal for small projects, experimentation, or learning AWS.

AWS Pricing Model

- **Pay-As-You-Go**:

- Charges based on actual resource usage (compute hours, storage capacity, etc.).

- Example: You only pay for the data you store on S3 or the time your EC2 instance runs.

- **Savings Plans**:

  - Discounts for committing to long-term usage (e.g., Reserved Instances for EC2).

- **Tiered Pricing**:

  - Costs decrease as usage increases (e.g., data transfer or storage).

- **Budget Management Tools**:

  - AWS Cost Explorer helps users predict and control costs.

Chapter 3: Setting Up AWS

3.1 Step-by-Step Guide to Creating an AWS Account

1. **Navigate to the AWS Homepage**:

   o   Visit https://aws.amazon.com and click **Create an AWS Account**.

2. **Enter Your Details**:

   o   Provide an email address, choose a password, and set an account name (e.g., "My Cloud Learning").

3. **Billing Information**:

   o   Add credit/debit card details.

   o   Note: AWS uses the card to verify your identity; charges may occur if usage exceeds the Free Tier.

4. **Identity Verification**:

   o   Enter your phone number for a one-time verification code.

5. **Choose a Support Plan**:

- Select the **Basic Support Plan** (free and sufficient for most users).

6. **Sign In to AWS**:

   - Use your credentials to access the AWS Management Console.

7. **Set Up Multi-Factor Authentication (MFA)**:

   - For enhanced security, enable MFA by:

     - Navigating to the **IAM Dashboard**.

     - Following the steps to link an authenticator app (e.g., Google Authenticator).

3.2 Understanding the AWS Management Console

Introduce readers to the central hub for managing AWS resources.

1. **What is the AWS Management Console?**

   - A web-based interface to provision and manage AWS services.

   - Visualize resources across multiple Regions and services.

2. **Navigating the Console**:

   - **Search Bar**: Quickly locate services (e.g., EC2, S3).

- o **Service Categories**:
  - Compute (e.g., EC2, Lambda).
  - Storage (e.g., S3, EBS).
  - Databases (e.g., RDS, DynamoDB).
- o **Account Dropdown**:
  - Access billing information, support, and security credentials.

3. **Hands-On Exercise**:
   - o Explore the dashboard, find **S3**, and note available Regions.

4. **Tips for Beginners**:
   - o Use the **Resource Groups** feature to organize your projects.
   - o Leverage the **Recently Visited Services** for quicker navigation.

3.3 Exploring AWS CLI and SDKs for Automation

What is AWS CLI?

- A command-line tool for managing AWS resources programmatically.

- Example: Instead of clicking through the Management Console, you can create an S3 bucket with a single command.

Setting Up AWS CLI:

1. **Installation**:
   - Download from AWS CLI Downloads.
   - Follow the setup instructions for your OS (Windows, macOS, or Linux).

2. **Configuration**:
   - Run the command:

bash

aws configure

   - Provide:
     - Access Key ID
     - Secret Access Key
     - Default Region (e.g., us-east-1)
     - Default output format (e.g., json)

3. **Verify Installation**:
   - Test the setup with:

bash

aws s3 ls

What are AWS SDKs?

- SDKs allow developers to interact with AWS services directly from programming languages (e.g., Python, Java, Node.js).

- Example Use Case: Upload files to S3 using a Python script.

Installing an SDK (Python Example):

1. **Install boto3**:

   o Run:

bash

```
pip install boto3
```

2. **Basic Script**:

   o Example: List all S3 buckets.

python

```
import boto3

s3 = boto3.client('s3')
response = s3.list_buckets()
print("Existing buckets:")
for bucket in response['Buckets']:
    print(f"  {bucket['Name']}")
```

3.4 Real-World Example: Setting Up a Simple S3 Bucket

What is S3?

- **Amazon Simple Storage Service (S3)** is a highly durable, scalable cloud storage service.

Creating an S3 Bucket:

Using the AWS Management Console:

1. **Navigate to S3**:

   o Search for **S3** in the console.

2. **Create a Bucket**:

   o Click **Create Bucket**.

   o Enter a unique bucket name (e.g., my-first-s3-bucket-123).

   o Choose a Region (e.g., us-east-1).

3. **Set Permissions**:

   o For now, leave the bucket private (default setting).

4. **Create**:

   o Click **Create Bucket**.

Using AWS CLI: Run the command:

bash

aws s3 mb s3://my-first-s3-bucket-123 --region us-east-1

Uploading a File to S3:

1. **From the Console**:

   o Open the bucket, click **Upload**, and select a file from your computer.

2. **Using AWS CLI**:

   o Run:

bash

```
aws s3 cp myfile.txt s3://my-first-s3-bucket-123/
```

3. **Verify**:

   o Check the file in the Management Console or list bucket contents using:

bash

```
aws s3 ls s3://my-first-s3-bucket-123/
```

Chapter 5: Deploying Your First Application

5.1 Setting Up a Web Server with EC2 and Load Balancing

What is Amazon EC2?

Amazon Elastic Compute Cloud (EC2) provides scalable virtual servers, enabling users to run applications without the need for physical hardware.

Step-by-Step Guide: Setting Up a Web Server

1. **Launch an EC2 Instance**:
    - Open the AWS Management Console and navigate to **EC2**.
    - Click **Launch Instance**.
    - Choose the Amazon Linux AMI or Ubuntu (Free Tier eligible).
    - Select the **t2.micro** instance type.
    - Configure:
        - Key Pair: Create or use an existing key pair for SSH access.

- Security Group: Open port 22 (SSH) and 80 (HTTP).
    - Launch the instance.
2. **Connect to the Instance**:
    - Use an SSH client or AWS Systems Manager Session Manager:

bash

```
ssh -i "your-key.pem" ec2-user@your-ec2-public-ip
```

3. **Install a Web Server**:
    - Update the package manager:

bash

```
sudo yum update -y
```

    - Install Apache or Nginx:

bash

```
sudo yum install httpd -y
sudo systemctl start httpd
sudo systemctl enable httpd
```

    - Place a test file in the web root:

bash

echo "Hello, AWS!" > /var/www/html/index.html

4. **Access the Web Server**:

   o Visit your EC2 instance's public IP in a browser (http://your-ec2-public-ip).

Adding Load Balancing with Elastic Load Balancer (ELB)

1. **Set Up an Application Load Balancer**:

   o Navigate to **EC2 Dashboard > Load Balancers**.

   o Create a new load balancer, specifying:

     ▪ Type: Application Load Balancer.

     ▪ Listener: HTTP (Port 80).

     ▪ Target Group: Add your EC2 instance to the target group.

2. **Test the Load Balancer**:

   o Use the load balancer's DNS name to access the web server.

   o Benefit: Handles traffic distribution and ensures high availability.

5.2 Deploying an Application Using AWS Elastic Beanstalk

What is Elastic Beanstalk?

Elastic Beanstalk simplifies deploying, managing, and scaling applications. It handles the underlying infrastructure (EC2, Load Balancers, etc.) while you focus on your application.

Step-by-Step Guide: Deploying a Sample Application

1. **Prepare Your Application**:
    - Use a simple Node.js, Python, or Java web application.
    - Example Node.js app:

javascript

```
const express = require('express');

const app = express();

app.get('/', (req, res) => res.send('Hello, Elastic Beanstalk!'));

app.listen(3000, () => console.log('App running on port 3000'));
```

2. **Zip the Application Files**:
    - Compress your application into a .zip file.

3. **Create a New Elastic Beanstalk Environment**:

- Navigate to **Elastic Beanstalk** in the AWS Management Console.

- Click **Create New Application**.

- Specify:

  - Platform: Choose the relevant runtime (e.g., Node.js).

  - Environment: Web server environment.

  - Application Code: Upload your .zip file.

4. **Monitor the Deployment**:

   - Elastic Beanstalk will automatically deploy your application and provide a public URL.

5. **Scale and Monitor**:

   - Use the **Environment Dashboard** to scale instances, monitor health, and configure alarms.

5.3 Real-World Example: Deploying a Static Website Using S3 and CloudFront

What is Amazon S3?

Amazon S3 is ideal for hosting static websites due to its high durability and low cost.

What is CloudFront?

CloudFront is AWS's content delivery network (CDN), accelerating website performance by caching content closer to users.

Step-by-Step Guide: Deploying a Static Website

1. **Host the Website on S3**:
   - Create an S3 bucket:
     - Bucket Name: Must be globally unique (e.g., my-static-website-123).
     - Region: Choose a nearby Region.
   - Enable Static Website Hosting:
     - Go to **Properties > Static Website Hosting**.
     - Specify:
       - Index document: index.html.
       - (Optional) Error document: error.html.
   - Upload Your Website Files:
     - Upload index.html, styles.css, etc., to the bucket.
     - Set files to **public** via bucket permissions.

2. **Test the S3 Website**:

- Use the bucket's public URL to view the website.

3. **Add CloudFront for Speed and Security**:

   - Navigate to **CloudFront** and create a new distribution:
     - Origin Domain: Your S3 bucket's website endpoint.
     - Viewer Protocol Policy: Redirect HTTP to HTTPS.
   - CloudFront will generate a public URL for your website.
   - Benefit: Faster load times and SSL encryption.

Chapter 6: Security in AWS

6.1 Introduction to Identity and Access Management (IAM)

What is IAM?

- **Identity and Access Management (IAM)** enables control over who can access AWS resources and what actions they can perform.

Key Components of IAM:

1. **Users**:
    - Individual accounts for team members.
    - Example: Developers, administrators, and testers.

2. **Groups**:
    - Collections of users sharing the same permissions.
    - Example: A "Developers" group might have access to EC2 and S3 but not billing.

3. **Roles**:

- Temporary permissions for AWS resources or external entities.

- Example: A Lambda function role allowing it to access an S3 bucket.

4. **Policies**:

- JSON documents defining permissions.

- Example: A policy granting "read-only" access to S3:

json

```
{
  "Version": "2012-10-17",
  "Statement": [
    {
      "Effect": "Allow",
      "Action": "s3:GetObject",
      "Resource": "arn:aws:s3:::example-bucket/*"
    }
  ]
}
```

Best Practices for IAM:

- **Principle of Least Privilege**:

- o Grant only the minimum permissions required.

- **Enable Multi-Factor Authentication (MFA)**:

  - o Add a second authentication layer for critical accounts.

- **Use IAM Roles**:

  - o Avoid sharing long-term access keys. Use roles wherever possible.

- **Audit Regularly**:

  - o Use **IAM Access Analyzer** to review permissions and identify unnecessary access.

Hands-On Example: Creating a User and Group

1. Navigate to the **IAM Console**.

2. Create a Group:

   - o Name: Developers.

   - o Attach the AmazonS3FullAccess policy.

3. Add a User:

   - o Name: JohnDoe.

   - o Assign to the Developers group.

4. Provide the user with console and programmatic access, noting their credentials.

6.2 Securing Data with Encryption

Why Encrypt Data?

Encryption ensures that even if data is intercepted or accessed by unauthorized individuals, it remains unreadable without the proper keys.

AWS Encryption Tools:

1. **AWS Key Management Service (KMS)**:

   o Centralized service for creating and managing cryptographic keys.

   o Use Cases:

      ▪ Encrypt sensitive data in applications.

      ▪ Encrypt S3 objects and database entries.

   o Example: Encrypting an S3 bucket using a KMS-managed key.

2. **S3 Encryption**:

   o S3 offers multiple encryption methods:

      ▪ **Server-Side Encryption (SSE)**:

         ▪ SSE-S3: AWS manages the encryption keys.

         ▪ SSE-KMS: AWS KMS manages the keys.

- **Client-Side Encryption**:
    - Data is encrypted before being uploaded to S3.
  - Enable encryption during S3 bucket creation.

Hands-On Example: Enabling S3 Encryption

1. Navigate to the **S3 Console**.

2. Select a bucket or create a new one.

3. Go to the **Properties** tab and enable **Default Encryption**:
   - Choose either **SSE-S3** or **SSE-KMS**.

4. Upload a file and verify its encrypted state in the bucket settings.

Encrypting Data in Transit:

- Use HTTPS for secure communication between clients and AWS resources.

- Example: Enforce HTTPS on a CloudFront distribution serving content from an S3 bucket.

6.3 Real-World Example: Managing User Access for a Small Development Team

Scenario:

A small startup has three types of users:

1. **Developers**: Need access to EC2 and S3.

2. **Finance Team**: Need access to billing information.

3. **Administrator**: Full access to manage resources.

Solution Using IAM:

1. **Define Groups and Policies**:

   o Developers:

      ▪ Policy: AmazonS3FullAccess and AmazonEC2FullAccess.

   o Finance:

      ▪ Policy: AWSBillingReadOnlyAccess.

   o Administrator:

      ▪ Policy: AdministratorAccess.

2. **Create Users and Assign Groups**:

   o Add individual accounts for each team member.

o   Assign users to their respective groups for consistent permissions.

3. **Enable MFA for Administrator Accounts**:

   o   Use MFA to protect high-privilege accounts.

4. **Regularly Audit Access**:

   o   Use **IAM Access Analyzer** to review policies.

   o   Rotate credentials every 90 days.

Outcome:

- **Improved Security**: Fine-grained control over who can access what.

- **Team Efficiency**: Users can perform their tasks without risk of overstepping boundaries.

- **Auditability**: Clear logs of who accessed or modified resources.

Chapter 7: Scaling Applications

7.1 Auto Scaling Groups and Elastic Load Balancers

What is Auto Scaling?

Auto Scaling allows applications to scale dynamically by automatically adjusting the number of instances based on demand.

Key Features of Auto Scaling:

1. **Dynamic Scaling**: Adds or removes instances based on real-time metrics like CPU utilization.

2. **Predictive Scaling**: Anticipates traffic patterns and adjusts resources proactively.

3. **Cost Efficiency**: Ensures resources match demand, avoiding over-provisioning.

Step-by-Step Guide: Setting Up an Auto Scaling Group

1. **Launch a Template Instance**:

- Set up a baseline EC2 instance (e.g., Ubuntu with a web server) and create an Amazon Machine Image (AMI).

2. **Create an Auto Scaling Group**:

   - Navigate to the **EC2 Console** > **Auto Scaling Groups** > **Create Auto Scaling Group**.

   - Configure:

     - Launch Template: Use the AMI created earlier.

     - Desired Capacity: Number of instances to maintain (e.g., 2).

     - Minimum and Maximum Size: Define the range (e.g., 1 to 5).

     - Scaling Policies:

       - Example: Add instances when CPU utilization exceeds 70%.

3. **Attach a Load Balancer**:

   - Use an Application Load Balancer (ALB) to distribute traffic across instances.

4. **Test Scaling**:

   - Simulate traffic to observe instances scaling up or down.

What is an Elastic Load Balancer (ELB)?

An Elastic Load Balancer distributes incoming traffic across multiple targets (EC2 instances, containers, or IP addresses) to ensure high availability.

Benefits of ELB:

1. **Traffic Distribution**: Prevents overloading a single instance.

2. **Health Checks**: Automatically routes traffic to healthy instances.

3. **Types of Load Balancers**:

   o **Application Load Balancer (ALB)**: Best for HTTP/HTTPS applications.

   o **Network Load Balancer (NLB)**: Low latency, suited for TCP traffic.

   o **Gateway Load Balancer (GLB)**: Ideal for integrating with third-party virtual appliances.

Hands-On Example: Setting Up a Load Balancer

1. Navigate to the **EC2 Console > Load Balancers**.

2. Create an ALB:

   o Listener: HTTP on port 80.

   o Target Group: Add your EC2 instances.

3. Test the setup:

     o   Access the application using the load
         balancer's DNS name.

7.2 Understanding AWS Regions and Availability Zones

What are AWS Regions?

AWS Regions are geographic locations where AWS data
centers are grouped. Each Region operates independently
for compliance and performance optimization.

Why Are Regions Important?

1. **Data Residency**: Some organizations need to store
   data in specific countries to comply with
   regulations.

2. **Latency Optimization**: Users experience lower
   latency when resources are hosted in nearby
   Regions.

3. **Disaster Recovery**: Distributing resources across
   Regions enhances fault tolerance.

What are Availability Zones (AZs)?

AZs are isolated locations within a Region, each with its
own power, networking, and cooling infrastructure.

Best Practices for Using Regions and AZs:

1. **Distribute Resources Across AZs**:

    o   Use multiple AZs for high availability.

    o   Example: Host EC2 instances in two AZs and use an ALB to route traffic.

2. **Region Selection**:

    o   Choose a Region close to your primary user base.

    o   Consider Regions with the required services (e.g., not all Regions support every AWS service).

3. **Cross-Region Replication**:

    o   Use S3 Cross-Region Replication to duplicate data in another Region for disaster recovery.

Hands-On Example: Multi-AZ Deployment

1. Launch EC2 instances in two AZs within the same Region.

2. Attach them to an ALB to distribute traffic.

3. Simulate AZ failure by stopping one instance and observe the load balancer redirecting traffic.

7.3 Real-World Example: Scaling an E-Commerce Platform During Peak Traffic

Scenario:

An e-commerce platform experiences traffic spikes during flash sales or seasonal promotions.

Solution Using AWS Tools:

1. **Auto Scaling for Backend Servers**:
   - Set up an Auto Scaling Group to add instances when CPU usage exceeds 75%.
   - Use predictive scaling to handle expected traffic surges during events like Black Friday.

2. **Elastic Load Balancer for Traffic Management**:
   - Distribute user traffic across multiple AZs to ensure availability.

3. **CloudFront for Static Assets**:
   - Serve images, CSS, and JavaScript files via Amazon CloudFront to reduce server load.

4. **Database Scaling**:
   - Use Amazon RDS with Read Replicas to handle high read traffic.

- o Scale vertically by increasing the instance size or horizontally by adding replicas.

5. **Monitoring and Alerts**:

   - o Use Amazon CloudWatch to set alarms for metrics like response time and instance count.

   - o Trigger notifications to the operations team during anomalies.

Outcome:

- During a flash sale, the platform scales up resources dynamically, maintaining performance and user experience.

- After the traffic spike, resources scale down, ensuring cost efficiency.

Chapter 8: Monitoring and Logging

8.1 Using AWS CloudWatch for Monitoring Resources

What is AWS CloudWatch?

AWS CloudWatch is a monitoring service that provides data and actionable insights for AWS resources and applications. It helps track performance metrics, set alarms, and visualize trends.

Core Features of CloudWatch:

1. **Metrics**:
   - Collect real-time data from AWS services like EC2, Lambda, and RDS.
   - Example: CPU utilization, memory usage, or disk I/O.

2. **Alarms**:
   - Notify users when a threshold is breached.
   - Example: Trigger an alarm if EC2 CPU utilization exceeds 80%.

3. **Dashboards**:

   o Create visual representations of metrics for easy monitoring.

4. **Logs**:

   o Collect, monitor, and analyze log data from applications and AWS services.

5. **Events**:

   o Automate responses to changes in your resources (e.g., restart an EC2 instance if it fails).

Step-by-Step Guide: Monitoring with CloudWatch

1. **View Metrics**:

   o Navigate to the **CloudWatch Console** > **Metrics**.

   o Select a service (e.g., EC2) and view metrics like CPU utilization.

2. **Create an Alarm**:

   o Go to **Alarms** > **Create Alarm**.

   o Set the metric (e.g., EC2 CPU Utilization > 75%).

   o Configure actions, like sending an email using Amazon SNS.

3. **Set Up a Dashboard**:

   o Go to **Dashboards** > **Create Dashboard**.

- o Add widgets to track critical metrics like Lambda execution time or S3 requests.

8.2 Logging with AWS CloudTrail

What is AWS CloudTrail?

CloudTrail is a service that logs API calls and user actions in your AWS account, providing an audit trail for security and troubleshooting.

Key Features of CloudTrail:

1. **Event Logging**:
   - o Logs API calls made via the AWS Console, CLI, SDKs, and other services.
   - o Example: Track who terminated an EC2 instance.

2. **Event History**:
   - o Access recent events directly in the CloudTrail Console.

3. **Trails**:
   - o Create trails to deliver logs to an S3 bucket for long-term storage or further analysis.

4. **Integration with Other Tools**:
   - o Integrate with CloudWatch for real-time monitoring of specific events.

Step-by-Step Guide: Setting Up CloudTrail

1. **Enable CloudTrail**:

   o Navigate to the **CloudTrail Console** > **Trails** > **Create Trail**.

   o Name your trail and select an S3 bucket for log storage.

2. **View Event History**:

   o Access recent API activity from the **Event History** tab.

3. **Search for Specific Events**:

   o Filter by service, event name, or user to find actions like "StartInstances" or "DeleteBucket".

8.3 Real-World Example: Detecting and Resolving Issues with a Lambda Function

Scenario:

A Lambda function processing orders in an e-commerce platform is intermittently failing, causing delayed order updates.

Using CloudWatch to Diagnose Issues:

1. **Access CloudWatch Logs**:
   - Navigate to **CloudWatch Console** > **Logs**.
   - Find the log group associated with the Lambda function.

2. **Analyze Logs**:
   - Review execution logs to identify errors.
   - Example: An error might indicate an issue with an API call or resource permissions.

3. **Monitor Metrics**:
   - Check metrics like **Invocation Count** and **Error Rate**.
   - Example: A spike in the error rate signals a recurring issue.

4. **Set Up an Alarm**:
   - Create a CloudWatch Alarm for the **Error Rate** metric.
   - Configure it to send a notification if errors exceed a threshold.

Using CloudTrail to Investigate:

1. **Track API Activity**:
   - Use CloudTrail to identify recent changes to the Lambda function or associated resources.

- o Example: A policy change might have removed necessary permissions.

2. **Correlate Events**:

   - o Combine logs from CloudWatch and CloudTrail to pinpoint the root cause.

Resolving the Issue:

- Adjust the Lambda function's IAM role to ensure proper permissions.

- Add error handling in the function code to retry failed operations.

- Test the function with sample data to confirm the fix.

Chapter 9: Serverless Architecture with AWS

9.1 What is Serverless Computing?

Definition:

Serverless computing allows developers to run applications and services without provisioning or managing servers. AWS handles infrastructure, scaling, and maintenance, enabling developers to focus on code and logic.

Key Characteristics:

1. **No Server Management**:

     o   AWS abstracts server infrastructure. Developers deploy functions, not servers.

2. **Event-Driven**:

     o   Functions are triggered by events (e.g., an HTTP request or file upload).

3. **Automatic Scaling**:

     o   Scale up or down based on demand, ensuring cost efficiency.

4. **Pay-as-You-Go**:

- Billing is based on execution time and resource usage, not idle server time.

Benefits:

- Reduced operational complexity.

- Lower costs for sporadic workloads.

- Faster time to market for applications.

Use Cases:

- Real-time file processing (e.g., image resizing on S3 uploads).

- Backend for web or mobile applications.

- IoT data ingestion and processing.

9.2 Building Applications with AWS Lambda, API Gateway, and DynamoDB

---

1. AWS Lambda

Lambda is AWS's compute service for running code in response to events.

- **Key Features**:
  - Supports multiple runtimes (Python, Node.js, Java, etc.).
  - Integrates seamlessly with other AWS services.
  - Executes code in response to triggers (e.g., S3 uploads, HTTP requests).
- **Example Use Case**:
  - A Lambda function processes data uploaded to S3 and writes it to DynamoDB.

---

2. Amazon API Gateway

API Gateway allows developers to create and manage RESTful APIs to expose Lambda functions to external users or applications.

- **Key Features**:
  - Create HTTP endpoints to trigger Lambda functions.
  - Handle authentication and authorization (e.g., with AWS Cognito or IAM).
  - Scale automatically to handle millions of requests.
- **Example Use Case**:
  - An API Gateway endpoint accepts client requests, passes them to a Lambda function, and returns processed data.

3. Amazon DynamoDB

DynamoDB is AWS's fully managed NoSQL database designed for high availability and low latency.

- **Key Features**:
    - Serverless, scales automatically.
    - Supports key-value and document-based data models.
    - Offers strong consistency and fine-grained security.
- **Example Use Case**:
    - Storing and retrieving user data for a serverless application.

9.3 Real-World Example: A Simple Serverless REST API

Scenario:

Create a serverless API for managing a to-do list. Users can add, view, and delete tasks.

Step-by-Step Guide:

Step 1: Create a DynamoDB Table

1. Navigate to the **DynamoDB Console**.

2. Create a table:

   o   Table Name: ToDoTable.

   o   Partition Key: TaskId (String).

3. Enable on-demand capacity for automatic scaling.

Step 2: Write Lambda Functions

1. Create a Lambda function for each API operation:

   o   **AddTask**:

       ▪   Inserts a new item into the
           ToDoTable.

   o   **GetTasks**:

       ▪   Retrieves all items from the
           ToDoTable.

   o   **DeleteTask**:

       ▪   Deletes an item by TaskId.

2. Example: AddTask Function (Python)

python

```
import boto3
import json
import uuid
```

```python
dynamodb = boto3.resource('dynamodb')
table = dynamodb.Table('ToDoTable')

def lambda_handler(event, context):
    task_id = str(uuid.uuid4())
    task = event['body']['task']

    table.put_item(Item={
        'TaskId': task_id,
        'Task': task
    })

    return {
        'statusCode': 200,
        'body': json.dumps({'TaskId': task_id, 'Task': task})
    }
```

Step 3: Set Up API Gateway

1. Navigate to the **API Gateway Console**.
2. Create a new REST API:
   - Name: ToDoAPI.
3. Define resources and methods:

- **POST /tasks** → Trigger AddTask Lambda.

- **GET /tasks** → Trigger GetTasks Lambda.

- **DELETE /tasks/{id}** → Trigger DeleteTask Lambda.

4. Deploy the API:

   - Create a new stage (e.g., dev).

   - Obtain the API Gateway URL.

Step 4: Test the API

1. Use tools like Postman or curl to test:

   - Add a task:

bash

```
curl -X POST https://{api-gateway-url}/tasks \
-H "Content-Type: application/json" \
-d '{"task": "Learn AWS"}'
```

   - Get all tasks:

bash

```
curl -X GET https://{api-gateway-url}/tasks
```

   - Delete a task:

bash

```
curl -X DELETE https://{api-gateway-url}/tasks/{TaskId}
```

Step 5: Monitor with CloudWatch

- Check logs for Lambda execution in the
  CloudWatch Logs Console.

- Set up CloudWatch Alarms for API errors or high
  latency.

Chapter 10: AWS for Developers

Goal

Empower readers to utilize AWS tools and best practices specifically tailored for developers. This chapter explores AWS SDKs for programming languages, continuous integration/continuous deployment (CI/CD) with AWS CodePipeline and CodeDeploy, and a hands-on example of automating deployments.

10.1 AWS SDKs for Python, Java, and Node.js

What Are AWS SDKs?

AWS SDKs (Software Development Kits) simplify the integration of AWS services into applications by providing language-specific libraries.

Popular SDKs and Their Features:

1. **Python (Boto3)**:
   - o Ideal for scripting and automation.
   - o Easy-to-use interface for interacting with AWS services.
   - o Example:

python

```
import boto3
s3 = boto3.client('s3')
response = s3.list_buckets()
print("Existing buckets:")
for bucket in response['Buckets']:
    print(f" {bucket['Name']}")
```

2. **Java (AWS SDK for Java)**:
   - o Offers robust, enterprise-grade capabilities.
   - o Useful for building scalable web applications.
   - o Example:

java

```
AmazonS3 s3Client = AmazonS3ClientBuilder.defaultClient();
List<Bucket> buckets = s3Client.listBuckets();
```

```
for (Bucket bucket : buckets) {

    System.out.println(bucket.getName());

}
```

3. **Node.js (AWS SDK for JavaScript)**:
    - Excellent for building real-time web applications and APIs.
    - Leverages JavaScript's asynchronous nature.
    - Example:

javascript

```javascript
const AWS = require('aws-sdk');
const s3 = new AWS.S3();
s3.listBuckets((err, data) => {
    if (err) console.log(err, err.stack);
    else console.log(data.Buckets);
});
```

When to Use SDKs:

- Automating tasks (e.g., creating EC2 instances, uploading files to S3).
- Building backend services for applications.
- Integrating with AWS resources programmatically.

10.2 CodePipeline and CodeDeploy for CI/CD

What is CI/CD?

- **Continuous Integration (CI)**: Automatically test and merge code changes into a shared repository.

- **Continuous Deployment (CD)**: Automatically deploy tested changes to production environments.

AWS CodePipeline:

CodePipeline automates the release process, from code changes to deployment.

- **Features**:

    o Integrates with GitHub, AWS CodeCommit, and other repositories.

    o Supports multiple stages (build, test, deploy).

    o Triggers actions based on code changes.

- **Example Workflow**:

    o A commit to GitHub triggers a build in AWS CodeBuild, followed by deployment via CodeDeploy.

AWS CodeDeploy:

CodeDeploy automates application deployments to EC2 instances, Lambda, or on-premises servers.

- **Features**:
    - o Supports rolling, blue/green, and canary deployment strategies.
    - o Integrates with CloudWatch to monitor deployment health.
- **Example**:
    - o Deploying a web application to an Auto Scaling group with zero downtime using a rolling update strategy.

10.3 Real-World Example: Automating Deployments with AWS CodePipeline

Scenario:

You want to automate the deployment of a Node.js web application hosted on an EC2 instance.

Step-by-Step Guide:

Step 1: Set Up the Application

1. Create a Node.js application and store the code in GitHub or AWS CodeCommit.

   o Example app.js:

javascript

```
const express = require('express');

const app = express();

app.get('/', (req, res) => res.send('Hello, CodePipeline!'));

app.listen(3000, () => console.log('App running on port 3000'));
```

2. Create an EC2 instance and configure it as the deployment target:

   o Install Node.js and dependencies.

   o Configure the instance with an IAM role for CodeDeploy access.

Step 2: Create a CodeDeploy Deployment Group

1. Navigate to the **CodeDeploy Console**.

2. Create an application:

   o Name: NodeAppDeploy.

3. Create a deployment group:

   o Add the EC2 instance(s) as targets.

   o Use the default CodeDeploy agent for deployments.

Step 3: Set Up CodePipeline

1. Navigate to the **CodePipeline Console** and create a pipeline:

    o Source Stage:

        ▪ Choose your repository (GitHub, CodeCommit).

        ▪ Specify the branch to monitor for changes.

    o Build Stage:

        ▪ Use AWS CodeBuild to test and package the application.

        ▪ Create a buildspec file (buildspec.yml) to define build instructions:

yaml

version: 0.2

phases:

 install:

  commands:

   - npm install

 build:

  commands:

```
      - npm run build
artifacts:
  files:
    - '**/*'
```

     o   Deploy Stage:

         ■   Use CodeDeploy to deploy the application to the EC2 instance.

Step 4: Test the Pipeline

1. Push a change to the repository (e.g., modify app.js).

2. Observe CodePipeline triggering the build and deployment stages.

3. Verify the deployed application:

   o Access the EC2 instance's public IP to confirm the update.

Step 5: Monitor and Optimize

- Use CloudWatch to monitor deployment health.

- Configure alarms for failed deployments or application errors.

Chapter 11: Cost Management and Optimization

11.1 AWS Cost Explorer and Budgets

What is AWS Cost Explorer?

AWS Cost Explorer is a tool for analyzing, visualizing, and managing AWS costs over time.

Key Features:

1. **Visualize Costs**:

   o View costs by service, linked accounts, or Regions.

   o Example: Determine how much you're spending on EC2 compared to S3.

2. **Forecast Spending**:

   o Use historical data to predict future costs.

3. **Set Up Cost Categories**:

   o Group services or projects into categories for granular tracking.

How to Use AWS Cost Explorer:

1. **Access Cost Explorer**:

   o Navigate to **Billing > Cost Explorer** in the AWS Management Console.

2. **Generate Reports**:

   o Filter by service, account, or usage type.

   o Example: Analyze daily spending on EC2 instances.

3. **Enable Resource-Level Tracking**:

   o Tag resources with labels like project, team, or environment.

   o View costs per project or team in Cost Explorer.

What are AWS Budgets?

AWS Budgets enable setting alerts for specific cost thresholds or usage limits.

How to Set Up a Budget:

1. **Navigate to AWS Budgets**:

   o Go to **Billing > Budgets**.

2. **Create a Budget**:

   - ○ Choose **Cost Budget** or **Usage Budget**.

   - ○ Example: Set a monthly budget of $100 for S3.

3. **Configure Alerts**:

   - ○ Define thresholds (e.g., 80% of the budget).

   - ○ Notify users via email or SNS when thresholds are exceeded.

11.2 Best Practices for Optimizing Costs

1. Use the Right Pricing Model:

- **On-Demand Instances**:

  - ○ Flexible but expensive for long-term use.

- **Reserved Instances (RIs)**:

  - ○ Commit to 1 or 3 years for significant savings.

  - ○ Example: Save up to 75% on EC2 costs.

- **Spot Instances**:

  - ○ Bid for unused capacity at lower prices.

  - ○ Ideal for batch processing or fault-tolerant workloads.

2. Right-Size Resources:

- **Monitor Resource Utilization**:
    - Use **AWS Compute Optimizer** to identify over-provisioned resources.

- Example:
    - Scale down an underutilized EC2 instance from m5.large to t3.medium.

---

3. Optimize Storage Costs:

- **S3 Storage Classes**:
    - Use **S3 Intelligent-Tiering** for automatic cost optimization.
    - Migrate infrequently accessed data to **S3 Glacier** for archival storage.

- Example:
    - Archive old log files in Glacier instead of Standard S3.

---

4. Leverage Free Tier:

- Monitor Free Tier usage to avoid exceeding limits.
- Example:
    - Ensure Lambda executions remain within the 1 million free requests/month.

5. Automate Cost Controls:

- **Turn Off Idle Resources**:

    o Automate stopping unused EC2 instances or RDS databases with Lambda.

- **Delete Unused Resources**:

    o Regularly clean up orphaned resources like unattached EBS volumes or unused Elastic IPs.

11.3 Real-World Example: Cost-Saving Tips for Startups

Scenario:

A startup is building a new mobile application and wants to minimize AWS costs during development.

Solution:

1. **Choose the Right Services**:

    o Use **AWS Lambda** instead of EC2 for backend APIs to avoid server costs.

o   Store app data in **Amazon DynamoDB** with on-demand capacity for low usage.

2. **Use Auto Scaling**:

    o   Configure Auto Scaling for EC2 instances to handle traffic spikes during testing.

3. **Enable Cost Monitoring**:

    o   Set up Cost Explorer to track daily expenses.

    o   Create a budget of $50/month to receive alerts if spending approaches the limit.

4. **Optimize Development Resources**:

    o   Turn off non-production environments after working hours using scheduled Lambda functions.

5. **Leverage Spot Instances**:

    o   Run testing workloads on Spot Instances to save up to 90%.

Outcome:

- The startup reduces development costs by 50%, reallocating savings to product improvements and marketing.

Chapter 12: Real-World Case Studies

12.1 AWS in E-Commerce

Use Case: Scaling for Seasonal Traffic

- **Challenge**:
    - E-commerce platforms face unpredictable traffic surges, especially during events like Black Friday or flash sales.

- **AWS Solution**:
    - **Auto Scaling**:
        - Automatically adjusts EC2 instances to handle high traffic volumes during sales and scales down during off-peak times.
    - **S3 and CloudFront**:
        - Serve product images and static content with minimal latency.
    - **RDS with Read Replicas**:
        - Handle high read traffic by distributing database queries across replicas.

- **Real-World Example**:
  - Shopify uses AWS to host its platform, allowing merchants to handle massive sales volumes seamlessly.

12.2 AWS in Healthcare

Use Case: Secure Data Storage and Analysis

- **Challenge**:
  - Healthcare providers need to securely store and analyze sensitive patient data while complying with regulations like HIPAA.

- **AWS Solution**:
  - **Amazon S3 with Encryption**:
    - Store patient records securely using encryption keys managed by AWS KMS.
  - **AWS Glue and Athena**:
    - Process and query large datasets for clinical research.
  - **Amazon SageMaker**:
    - Build machine learning models for predictive analytics, such as patient outcome forecasting.

- **Real-World Example**:

- Moderna used AWS to accelerate vaccine development by analyzing billions of genetic data points in secure cloud environments.

12.3 AWS in Fintech

Use Case: Building Scalable and Secure Payment Platforms

- **Challenge**:
  - Fintech companies require highly scalable infrastructure to handle financial transactions securely and reliably.

- **AWS Solution**:
  - **DynamoDB**:
    - Low-latency, serverless database for storing transaction data.
  - **AWS Shield and WAF**:
    - Protect against DDoS attacks and secure APIs.
  - **AWS Lambda and API Gateway**:
    - Enable serverless microservices architecture for payment processing.

- **Real-World Example**:

- Stripe leverages AWS to scale payment processing globally, ensuring seamless and secure transactions for millions of businesses.

12.4 Real-World Example: How Airbnb Optimizes Its Platform Using AWS

Challenge:

- Airbnb needed to scale globally to accommodate millions of users while maintaining high availability and fast performance.

AWS Solution:

1. **Compute**:

   - **Amazon EC2**:
     - Powers Airbnb's platform with scalable compute resources.

   - **Spot Instances**:
     - Reduces costs for fault-tolerant workloads like image processing.

2. **Storage**:

   - **Amazon S3**:

- Hosts property images and static assets, ensuring high durability and availability.

3. **Databases**:

   o **Amazon RDS**:

     - Scalable, managed relational databases for storing user and property data.

   o **Elasticache**:

     - Improves application response times by caching frequent queries.

4. **Machine Learning**:

   o **Amazon SageMaker**:

     - Builds recommendation systems for personalized user experiences.

5. **Global Availability**:

   o **CloudFront**:

     - Delivers content with low latency to users worldwide.

   o **Multi-Region Architecture**:

     - Ensures high availability and disaster recovery capabilities.

Outcome:

- Airbnb scales seamlessly during high-demand periods, such as holidays or major events.

- Users enjoy fast and reliable experiences regardless of their location.

Chapter 13: Preparing for AWS Certification

13.1 Overview of AWS Certification Paths

What Are AWS Certifications?

AWS certifications validate cloud expertise and knowledge of AWS services, boosting credibility and career opportunities.

Certification Levels:

AWS offers certifications at different levels, catering to varying roles and experience:

1. **Foundational**:

    o **AWS Certified Cloud Practitioner**:

        ▪ Target Audience: Beginners with little or no prior cloud experience.

        ▪ Focus: AWS basics, billing, and cloud concepts.

        ▪ Exam Duration: 90 minutes.

- Example Roles: Non-technical stakeholders, sales professionals.

2. **Associate**:

   o **AWS Certified Solutions Architect – Associate**:

     - Target Audience: Developers and architects building AWS-based solutions.

     - Focus: Designing distributed systems on AWS.

   o **AWS Certified Developer – Associate**:

     - Target Audience: Software developers.

     - Focus: Developing and deploying AWS applications.

   o **AWS Certified SysOps Administrator – Associate**:

     - Target Audience: System administrators.

     - Focus: Managing and operating AWS environments.

3. **Professional**:

   o **AWS Certified Solutions Architect – Professional**:

     - Focus: Advanced solutions design and architecture.

- AWS Certified DevOps Engineer – **Professional**:
  - Focus: CI/CD, automation, and security.

4. **Specialty**:
   - For advanced roles, certifications include:
     - Security
     - Data Analytics
     - Machine Learning
     - Advanced Networking

Choosing the Right Certification:

- **Beginners**: Start with **Cloud Practitioner** or **Solutions Architect – Associate**.

- **Developers**: Opt for **Developer – Associate**.

- **SysAdmins**: Pursue **SysOps Administrator – Associate**.

- **Advanced Professionals**: Progress to **Professional** or **Specialty** paths.

13.2 Study Tips and Resources

Tips for Preparing:

1. **Understand the Exam Blueprint**:

- Visit the AWS Certification website to review the domains and weightings.
- Example: Solutions Architect – Associate covers:
    - Domain 1: Design Resilient Architectures (30%).
    - Domain 2: Design Cost-Optimized Architectures (18%).

2. **Leverage AWS Free Tier**:
    - Gain hands-on experience with AWS services.
    - Example: Practice creating S3 buckets, setting up EC2 instances, and deploying Lambda functions.

3. **Take Practice Exams**:
    - Use official AWS practice tests or third-party platforms like Whizlabs or Udemy.

4. **Focus on Core Services**:
    - Master commonly used AWS services like EC2, S3, RDS, Lambda, and CloudFront.

5. **Join Study Groups**:
    - Participate in AWS certification forums or local meetups.

Recommended Resources:

1. **Official AWS Training**:
   - AWS provides training courses for each certification.
   - Example: "Architecting on AWS" for Solutions Architect – Associate.

2. **Whitepapers**:
   - Essential reads include the **Well-Architected Framework** and **Security Best Practices**.

3. **Online Platforms**:
   - **A Cloud Guru** and **Linux Academy**: Comprehensive certification courses.
   - **YouTube**: Free tutorials and exam walkthroughs.

4. **Documentation and FAQs**:
   - Read AWS service documentation to deepen understanding.

5. **Hands-On Labs**:
   - Use platforms like **Qwiklabs** or **Cloud Academy** for guided exercises.

13.3 Real-World Example: Benefits of Certification in Career Advancement

Case Study: John – From System Admin to Cloud Architect

1. **Background**:
   - John worked as a system administrator with no cloud experience.
   - He wanted to transition into cloud computing to stay relevant in a changing IT landscape.

2. **Journey**:
   - Started with the **AWS Certified Cloud Practitioner** to learn fundamentals.
   - Progressed to **Solutions Architect – Associate** for hands-on knowledge of AWS architecture.
   - Completed the **Solutions Architect – Professional** certification to demonstrate expertise.

3. **Outcome**:
   - John transitioned into a Cloud Architect role at a multinational company.
   - His salary increased by 35%, and he gained opportunities to lead cloud migration projects.

General Career Benefits of AWS Certifications:

1. **Increased Credibility**:

   o   Certifications validate skills, making you a stronger candidate for cloud-focused roles.

2. **Higher Salaries**:

   o   Certified professionals often earn higher compensation.

   o   Example: AWS Certified Solutions Architect – Associate averages $120,000/year.

3. **Broader Opportunities**:

   o   Certifications open doors to roles like Solutions Architect, DevOps Engineer, and Cloud Consultant.

4. **Networking**:

   o   Access to the **AWS Certified Global Community** and exclusive AWS events.

Chapter 14: Future of Cloud Computing and AWS

14.1 AI/ML Services in AWS

The Rise of AI/ML in Cloud Computing:

Artificial Intelligence (AI) and Machine Learning (ML) are revolutionizing industries by enabling predictive analytics, automation, and real-time decision-making. AWS provides tools and services that make AI/ML accessible to businesses of all sizes.

AWS AI/ML Services:

1. **Amazon SageMaker**:
   - A fully managed service for building, training, and deploying ML models.
   - Features:
     - Pre-built algorithms for common use cases.
     - SageMaker Studio: A unified IDE for ML development.

- Example: Build a recommendation system for e-commerce.

2. **AWS AI Services**:

   - **Amazon Rekognition**: Image and video analysis (e.g., facial recognition, object detection).

   - **Amazon Polly**: Text-to-speech service for creating lifelike voices.

   - **Amazon Comprehend**: Natural language processing for sentiment analysis and entity recognition.

   - **Amazon Lex**: Build conversational AI applications (chatbots) similar to Alexa.

3. **ML-Powered Analytics**:

   - **AWS Glue DataBrew**: Automate data preparation with AI.

   - **Amazon Forecast**: Generate accurate business forecasts using historical data.

Impact of AI/ML on Industries:

1. **Healthcare**:

   - Use AI to detect diseases like cancer through medical imaging.

   - Example: SageMaker enables faster training of diagnostic models.

2. **Retail**:

- o Personalize shopping experiences with AI-powered recommendations.

3. **Finance**:

- o Detect fraudulent transactions using real-time analytics.

14.2 AWS Outposts and Hybrid Cloud

What is Hybrid Cloud?

A hybrid cloud combines on-premises infrastructure with cloud services, enabling organizations to retain control over sensitive data while leveraging cloud scalability.

AWS Outposts:

AWS Outposts bring AWS infrastructure and services to on-premises environments.

- **Key Features**:
  - o Run AWS services like EC2, EBS, and RDS locally.
  - o Seamlessly integrate on-premises workloads with AWS Regions.
  - o Maintain low latency for applications requiring real-time processing.
- **Benefits**:

- Meet regulatory requirements by keeping data on-premises.

- Modernize legacy applications without full cloud migration.

Use Cases for Hybrid Cloud:

1. **Healthcare**:

   - Process sensitive patient data locally while leveraging AWS for large-scale analytics.

2. **Manufacturing**:

   - Real-time control systems require low-latency edge processing.

3. **Retail**:

   - Implement hybrid point-of-sale (POS) systems with centralized analytics in the cloud.

AWS's Vision for Hybrid Cloud:

With AWS Outposts, AWS aims to bridge the gap between on-premises and cloud, ensuring businesses can adopt modern technologies without compromising on compliance or performance.

14.3 Real-World Example: AWS Contributions to Autonomous Vehicles

Overview:

Autonomous vehicles (AVs) rely on massive computational power to process sensor data, train ML models, and make split-second decisions.

How AWS Powers Autonomous Vehicle Development:

1. **Data Storage and Processing**:

   o Autonomous vehicles generate terabytes of data daily from cameras, LiDAR, and radar.

   o **S3 and Glacier**:

     ▪ Store raw and historical data cost-effectively.

   o **AWS IoT Core**:

     ▪ Manage real-time vehicle telemetry.

2. **ML Training with SageMaker**:

   o Train and optimize deep learning models for object detection, path planning, and decision-making.

   o Example: Develop neural networks for traffic sign recognition.

3. **Simulation and Testing**:

   o **AWS RoboMaker**:

- Simulate autonomous vehicle environments for testing algorithms.
  - o Reduce time and costs associated with physical testing.

4. **Edge Computing with AWS Outposts**:
   - o Process real-time data from vehicles at the edge, minimizing latency.

Case Study: AWS and Zoox:

- **Challenge**:
  - o Zoox, an autonomous vehicle company, required a robust infrastructure for ML training and real-time data processing.

- **AWS Solution**:
  - o Used SageMaker for rapid ML model development.
  - o Leveraged AWS IoT for monitoring vehicle performance.
  - o Built scalable storage solutions with S3 for massive data ingestion.

- **Outcome**:
  - o Accelerated development cycles and reduced operational costs, bringing Zoox closer to deploying safe, reliable autonomous vehicles.

Chapter 15: Conclusion and Next Steps

15.1 Summarizing Key Learnings

As we conclude this journey through AWS and cloud computing, let's revisit the most important takeaways from each chapter:

1. **Understanding Cloud Computing**:

   - Cloud computing revolutionizes IT by offering scalable, cost-efficient, and globally accessible resources.

2. **Getting Started with AWS**:

   - AWS's wide range of services enables users to build, deploy, and manage applications with ease.

3. **Deploying and Managing Applications**:

   - From EC2 and Auto Scaling to Elastic Beanstalk and serverless solutions like Lambda, AWS provides flexible tools for every application type.

4. **Optimizing Security and Costs**:

- AWS ensures secure operations through IAM, encryption, and monitoring, while tools like Cost Explorer help manage spending.

5. **Real-World Impact**:
   - AWS drives innovation across industries, from e-commerce to healthcare, and powers futuristic applications like autonomous vehicles.

6. **Certification and Growth**:
   - AWS certifications validate skills and open doors to career advancement, making cloud computing an accessible and lucrative field.

15.2 Next Steps for Readers

As you close this book, here are actionable steps to continue your cloud journey:

---

1. Gain Hands-On Experience

- Sign up for the **AWS Free Tier** to practice:
  - Create EC2 instances, deploy a Lambda function, and set up an S3 bucket.
- Explore advanced scenarios like scaling applications with Auto Scaling or deploying APIs with API Gateway.

2. Pursue AWS Certifications

- Identify the certification path that aligns with your goals:

    - Beginners: Start with **AWS Certified Cloud Practitioner**.

    - Developers and Architects: Consider the **Solutions Architect – Associate** or **Developer – Associate**.

- Create a study plan and leverage resources like practice exams and whitepapers.

3. Build Real-World Projects

- Create a portfolio of AWS-based applications:

    - Deploy a static website using S3 and CloudFront.

    - Develop a serverless REST API with Lambda, API Gateway, and DynamoDB.

    - Use SageMaker to experiment with machine learning models.

4. Stay Updated on AWS Innovations

- AWS continuously evolves. Keep up with new services and features by:

    - Attending AWS events like **re**

.

- o Subscribing to AWS blogs and newsletters.

- o Participating in AWS user groups or forums.

5. Collaborate and Contribute

- Join the AWS community:

  - o Collaborate on open-source projects.

  - o Share your experiences through blog posts or YouTube tutorials.

- Networking can open opportunities and deepen your understanding.

15.3 Encouragement for the Journey Ahead

Cloud computing is more than just a skill—it's a doorway to innovation, problem-solving, and global impact. As you continue your learning journey:

- Embrace challenges; they're opportunities to grow.

- Stay curious and experiment with AWS services to uncover their full potential.

- Remember, the cloud is not just about technology—it's about transforming ideas into reality.

15.4 Final Reflection

Ask yourself:

- **What problem can I solve with cloud computing?**

- **How can I leverage AWS to advance my career or business goals?**

This is just the beginning of your cloud journey. With AWS as your platform and these learnings as your foundation, you're equipped to innovate, create, and lead in the digital era.

www.ingramcontent.com/pod-product-compliance
Lightning Source LLC
LaVergne TN
LVHW051715050326
832903LV00032B/4224